How to Be the Happiest Person You Know!

d|n a book by don nenninger

Table of Contents

Testimonials

"Don knows his happiness! If you want to be happier and healthier Don can help you today-he helped me, and my life has changed!"

"If you want personal coaching, if you want to change your life, if you want to make shifts, there is no one better to work with then Don. You can absolutely change your life; I know because I did. The best part, he didn't make me follow his path, he helped me to discover mine and that makes all the difference. If you want to make changes read his books—they're positive, filled with real tips that you can use, and non-judgmental. Bottom line-they helped me to live a happier and healthier life."

"Thank you for helping me to change my life."

"I was feeling so frustrated with my life-unhappy, blaming everybody for what I was dealing with— you can figure out that wasn't working! Did I say I was fat, fat, fat and unhappy! Finally, I figured what did I have to lose, so I talked with Don, honestly, I didn't know what to expect. It's hard, I was scared but I was sick of living that way. Patience, care, and helpful shifts moved me to a new experience of life. I feel better than ever before. Making the shift wasn't as hard as I feared; want to know what I found hard-everything about my life before I made the shift! Now, that was HARD!

How to Be the Happiest Person You Know:

People are happy as they make up their minds to be. ~Abraham Lincoln.

You are what you think you are. ~Buddha

When your experience of life consists of chronically low, depressed life energy you'll find that you rarely experience happiness. When you shift that energy, (and that's what this short book does), to a new state, you'll find and embrace vitality and life-balance. This shift results in an increase in your level of happiness.

Happiness Idea: You've got to understand that you're really in a battle for your soul. Right now, it's you vs. what society is trying to dictate to you as your path to happiness. The big problem with this battle is the battle lines are not clearly demarcated and built in favor of them. They use repetition, subconscious influence, superstars, aspirational and influential marketing and a host of other psychological techniques intentionally designed to bring you towards their desires and away from what we truly need to experience more genuine happiness.

Advertisers, politicians, religions and society relentlessly attempt to manipulate and imprint *their* messages on *your* subconscious to meet **their** needs. Make no mistake about it, this is a battle for your soul and billions of dollars are spent every year to convince you that popular culture has the answer as to why you're unsatisfied and unhappy.

You've got to inoculate yourself from this virus of material, consumer, social conditioning. You can't buy into the garbage they're selling! Even some religions invest tremendous amounts of time telling you all the sins you're guilty of and all the reasons for your trip to hell- unless of course you follow their path and you join with them. Now that's pressure!

Hey, their message and advertising plays upon our base instincts to be popular, well-liked, known, "selfie" that, "insta" that, buy this, sell that, vote for me, think like me~ or else!

But, do you ever consider what the unwritten cost of the "or else" would turn out to be? The "or else" is that when you try to follow the dictates of society without thinking and feeling for yourself you'll end up in a life of SRD (suppression, repression and denial/depression).

But, the truth is this, and remember this enormously important fact:

Happiness Idea: There is no external manifestation of anything that makes you more or less important, better or worse, or happy or sad~ to yourself.

Your emotions and internal emotional states are related to your perspective of what you have injected onto the past, present or future.

Thus, it's not the external that determines happiness. It's your judgements and evaluations of the external situation that determine your happiness, it's your thoughts and beliefs about every situation you experienced in your past, that you experience now, and that you believe you will experience in the future that determine your outlook and perspective.

Happiness Idea: The time is now for you to review and to take charge of these thoughts to see what impact they're having on your life.

Each emotional state that you live in; depression, joy, fear, love (and the many others) represent the result of your unrecognized judgment and evaluation of life. These thoughts/emotions reside within your internalized interpretation of prior life events that are projected into your present experience. These judgments are affected by your life history and your personal perception (bias)-in other words, today is the result of your perception of some event, not by the event itself.

Happiness Idea: Oh man, I hear the screaming now! You probably don't like hearing that you have some control! It's easier to blame. People have so much resistance to owing their personal contributions we make to our lives contained in this complex interaction of judgment, emotions, and evaluations of situations that affect our state of being.

Why Are Causes of Resistance to Change?

Happiness Idea: Sometimes a person is resistant because it's just so much easier to blame someone else, get angry at something, or use some dysfunctional coping behavior to hide our genuine emotion. Or, holding onto resentment provides them with some type of power or adrenaline.

Quite often though, they think that they have already spent so much time (sunk costs invested) that they're often waiting for the next "there" to arrive before they allow happiness- after all this could be the time. "There" could be a job, "there" could be a relationship, "there" could be getting out of a relationship- the "there" changes for each person, but they see happiness as something that happens to them from the outside.

Happiness Idea: Remember that happiness is not an outside-in paradigm; *happiness is always inside you waiting to be tapped, nurtured and encouraged in your life.*

Increasing your life energy and becoming balanced and harmonized are simple tools you can shift into using and these are tools you can develop. Using them is within your control. And, because they are in your control so is the possibility of experiencing more happiness!

Happiness Idea: Society will continually try to sell you that material items and external "things" are the key to happiness. The shift to happiness is not outward onto some external "thing" that will "make" you happy. The required shift is to loving yourself more, honoring yourself more, and increasing your energy so that you are looking at the world through a higher state of being- a different and more powerful reality.

The experience of allowing the flow of happiness is like looking though a different lens at the same scene- the scene is the same, but your view of the scene is changed by looking at it through a different lens. This higher state of being then allows the experience of happiness to flow more easily in your life.

Happiness Idea: So, to recap; you expand happiness in your life by shifting your awareness and balancing your energy flow.

Finally, A Happy Me!

Happiness Idea: *The side effects of this book will include an increased passion for life, love, & happiness!*

Each of us "knows" what we already know— *and that's all we know.* So for you to start embracing more happiness in life each of you must make shifts towards something different than what you already "know." Or not- that's a choice you have.

My experience- learned through three decades of work with clients of all types and my own journey, shows that when you begin to pay attention and emphasize some of the other things that you've overlooked in your life that's the time that you begin to develop a different experience. Doesn't that make sense? If you look at things the same way today as you did yesterday and the day before why would you expect to experience any change tomorrow? If you change the focus to gratitude and appreciation, you will experience more gratitude and appreciation, and you'll be happier. If not, you won't. The decision is up to you to walk through the door into the unknown.

Sometimes it's helpful to have a picture in your mind as a guide to help you move beyond the rational/critical mind into the all-encompassing holistic mind. Think of this book as providing you that picture- the picture of a doorway through an opening to a new place that some people will choose to walk through, and others will not.

Life is guaranteed to present different situations to us. Some of these life situations are frustrating, challenging and sad experiences. And, if we're not careful, we can start to believe that's all there is in life. In those moments, we often lose sight of the gift we are in the world, the gifts we bring to the world, and the gift we have- living today in this world.

Happiness Idea: How rare of a gift are you? Well, researchers calculated that the odds of your existence would be the equivalent of taking every grain of sand on earth on all the beaches of the world and reaching down and picking out one single grain out of that vastness. That's the gift of you.

You know, I've thought about how to best approach a subject that many people are curious about. They feel something is missing. Reading this book doesn't take long, let's say a couple hours at most, because I believe short and powerful beats long and boring every day! And, it's unrealistic to think that this book has every answer for everyone— but the ideas contained here are those that have worked for many clients and that are supported by research to bring more joy and happiness to you. These ideas are similar to the concepts of happiness that many religions and philosophies strive to teach in their messages, but the message gets lost.

I hope you enjoy this book and the cost you have to pay (we are always making energy exchanges) is an open mind and opening your heart. Look, if you feel resistant and you don't like the concepts presented here, you're still free to continue exactly what you've been doing. I want more for you. I want you to shift your mindset into one of appreciation and gratitude.

There's no criticism here. And, I don't want anything from you. I don't want you to sign up for some expensive program. My goal here is to share the learning that has helped me and others. In my life I am a teacher, and from my experience and work as a coach and counselor (who has worked with clients for decades) it has become clear what works and doesn't work to shift into happiness.

I have found that for me it's important to give back to the world in a way that has meaning for me. Help the world in each of our individual ways. By giving in this way I receive positive value out of the experience of writing this book as I hope you do too when reading it.

Happiness Idea: Are there shortcuts to experiencing more happiness in your life? No. If I could make a suggestion to you it would be to shift how you look at feelings and to stop judging them as "right" or "wrong" but to look at them as presenting valuable messages. Although I have strived to keep this book brief and readable this book represents years of evolving experience and incorporates the synthesis of years of therapy, training in psychology, (including as a school psychologist) and a life-time of interest and research. If the time is right for you, and it's meant to be, this book is a powerful tool that will resonate with your soul.

Happiness Idea: As an investment in your well-being, take some time to reflect, consider, and contemplate the small shifts outlined within the book. Don't just rush through the book to view it as another task checked off the list of never ending tasks.

Happiness Idea: It's an important step in the development of your whole, holistic person to occasionally take a moment to bring into your conscious awareness what thoughts you've *subconsciously chosen to lock onto*—and why are you locked into these particular thought patterns. Learn to challenge yourself to unravel what thoughts you've been accepting as everyday habit. That discovery is important! Discover what thoughts you're *locked* on to and why?

Have you ever considered what males up the real you? They are the thoughts you think. Where did these thoughts come from? When you consider the reasons why these thoughts feel like they are the "real" you, it's because, well, you have had these same thoughts for a long time and given them your energy and the repetition ingrained them. Some of this repetition is societal conditioning that you've internalized as your repetitive thought patterns. So, whether you realize this or not, "you" are simply patterned, habituated thoughts. You've had these thoughts for so long this just feels like the "real" you. And, these patterns can be replaced by more empowering thoughts which leads to more empowering actions.

You learn that by actively contemplating what your life can be like with a renewed perspective and different focus (mindset) that you'll walk a more interesting, fulfilling and yes, happier path.

Happiness Idea: Sometimes it feels like I've read almost every book on the psychology of happiness. Then worked with people for years who were deep in struggle. The message gleaned from this is: What's going to shift? Are they going to resist change? Will they continue to argue for their limitations to "prove" they're right?

I don't know what their justifications are for not choosing to live from a more powerful paradigm- I just hope they're not in the habit of arguing for their perceived limits.

There's not only one path to happiness. I don't believe your only chance to experience happiness would come to you in some epiphany, or by reading some "magical" 800-page book, or by encouraging you to go out and spend thousands of dollars in pursuit of something you already carry inside of you-the ability to experience far more happiness. That's not the message I believe and that's not what I want for you. Not only would you lose interest, you would probably feel more overwhelmed than inspired.

Just Start with Where You're at Today

If you are one of those people (and most of us are) who has been swamped by societal conditioning and who now endeavors to change the quality of their life by learning to make decisions from your heart-center you will learn to release that which needs releasing, nurture that which needs nurturing and you'll discover that the space for happiness is already inside you.

How do I know this? I've been with people who have experienced difficult life situations. I've worked with people who were so locked in their beliefs that they couldn't believe there were other ways to move through life. I want to share my compassion for any person who has experienced difficult life challenges because of trauma, PTSD, medical or mental health conditions, loss, and any other difficult trials.

The medical and mental health fields strive to help people suffering from these types of and there is hope for continuing progress. There's cutting edge research to help those who depression using treatments such as Ayahuasca, micro-dosing LSD, nutritional therapy, different energy modalities, therapies and much more. The search to provide relief for people who have sought answers for years.

But, there's also a malady that is not written about- SRD. SRD is the personal experience of suppression, repression and the resultant denial (depression) that we experience as individuals in a society that has lost its way. My hope is that for those of you who experience this disease (and I believe we all experience this to some degree) that this book may open another way for you to connect with alternative ways to experience happiness.

And, I'd like to suggest to you that even if find yourself in one of the states of depression/anger/suppression etc. that integrating the shifts in this book as a supplement to whatever treatment you choose may help you. In addition to the challenges noted above, you may also be experiencing some of the frustration and torment that comes from trying to somehow fit in life in a way you're not meant to- a toxic byproduct of SRD.

As you grow, and learn to honor your soul, you may discover that you don't really need to strive to fit in anymore— because you'll be happy with yourself and where you are. The detailed perspective shifts within will provide a benefit for you and provide the opening to make the shift to learn more, care more, and love yourself more.

Remember, you don't have to struggle anymore to fit into the square hole when you're a triangle!

Developing Heart Centered Success

Now, forget the nonsense that happiness comes from the outside in. What happens in the world will never determine your happiness.

Happiness Idea: Your *interpretation of those events will determine what you feel.* That interpretation is directly related to your mindset. The only rule I know of regarding happiness is that *no one's buying their way to happiness.* No matter what some guru says.

It is true that a little extra money does take the edge off the financial stressors of life. Living a life in survival mode is difficult. A little extra money helps get us to a place of financial safety. But, if you ask lotto winners who had millions of dollars gifted to them you would be surprised at how often an increase in expenses follows an increase in income! More people find themselves in the same financial wreck that they were in before! And, we're looking for more than simply income, we're looking for a truly holistic and happy soul. We want the true power and freedom found from living out the statement- "your path to happiness."

And, there's no heart-centered success in spending a fortune chasing happiness or buying into what the latest new guru is telling you- that you're doing happiness "wrong" and only they have the solution (which, of course, you can buy from them-for a lot of your money).

Happiness Idea: There's a funny expression I heard- recently after giving a talk-you know why so many people call themselves a guru? Because the word "charlatan" is easy to misspell!

A more balanced and long-lasting approach to happiness is to find your solution that revolves on finding *your path to your* happiness

Okay, that's it for the "rule," consider the rest of the book as suggestions, food for thought, and a collection of real methods that worked for real clients who wanted real change

Happiness Idea: Life is not changed, and happiness is not attained, by big dramatic theoretical shifts that you never put into practice in your life. Happiness is attained (and life is changed) by making incredibly small shifts that you actually put into action.

And making those tiny changes in your mindset- and well, you can do that! That's what this book is about. Throughout the book are simple ways to help you ignite the fuse of change to begin on your path to happiness!

Haven't you, over the years, seen the muck people are stuck in every day of their lives? Often, they stay in that same muck for years. It's obvious they're stuck to everyone- but them- that there's a problem.

Luckily, I've seen what works and I've seen what doesn't work to get people out of their muck. But I want to share something important.

Happiness Idea: There are people *who are not ready or willing to move out of their problems, attitudes and thoughts even though these are clearly not working for them.*

Some people really want to move beyond struggle in their lives. The want to *lean into* and embrace the naturally occurring feeling of happiness. In a nutshell, what many people want is to be happier. Still, some people don't- they just don't- and you must know where you are today to determine what you are willing to do.

Throughout my life there's been struggle, depression, tough life situations and brushes with the maker- isn't that true for you as well? Been in therapy, given therapy, and sat with people sharing the joy and sorrow in their soul.

Each of these experiences showed me how a modest shift in personal perspective, shifting one's beliefs, and becoming aware of what you focus on is the most powerful way to reconnect with the happiness already inside you.

Happiness Idea: And, this happiness is willing to shine when you commit to giving up the negative stories of the past and the drama that feels so real and so true today. That "truth" that you've been living is merely the reflection of what was in the past.

Imprinting and Introjects

Happiness Pont: Growing up each of us is swamped with negative subconscious imprinting called introjects. An introject is an unconsciously absorbed thought and/or behavior pattern that a person is exposed to and then internalizes.

When we're young we haven't developed an important part of our psyche- a part of our mind that contains what is called the "critical faculty." Because this has not yet formed, we are unable to discern whether what we are being exposed to is good for us. Thus, we accept the imprinting that we were exposed to good or bad.

So, where does this imprinting come from? This imprinting is put upon us from society, family, friends and an assortment of other sources. There are times when this imprinting is positive, and we benefit from life-enhancing behaviors. But, when this imprinting is negative, (or the imprinting is contrary to our nature), we end up living in the land of SRD- suppression, repression and the resulting denial/depression of the joy that could be in our life. That's the place where most people in our society exist today.

Happiness Idea: Your thought about you often represent the imprinting you've been exposed to previously. The thoughts are not the real you. They're simply not. These thoughts represent the amalgamation of the collective biases, beliefs, and contrived semantic heuristics shortcuts that we all carry and many times heuristic shortcuts that can do much more harm than good.

What is a heuristic shortcut? It's a shortcut we've developed over the years to speed up our assessment of a situation. We could spend years looking at all the data our brains collect but we would be so inefficient at living that survival would be doubtful.

By using shortcuts in our mind, we save some functional energy as we use the "good enough" assessment of situations to manage life. The problem? The shortcuts are often inaccurate and unhelpful to us dealing with the information of today and often lead us to where we have already been

Happiness Idea: When you grasp that concept, when you really "get" and truly understand that the habitual thoughts you have contribute to your diminished experience of life, that's when you open the door to change (this book opens that door and will help start the process of change).

So, starting today, please look for ways to ease into enjoying your life as you learn to surf the waves of life's ups and downs that we all must inevitably deal with.

Learn to embrace life's challenges from your soul. Your choice to ride *that* wave will make for a hell of a better ride!

You Bring Your Energy Wherever You Go.

Happiness Idea: The universal energy we live our lives in, the energy of the universe, is abundant. If there's lack in our life (including the lack of happiness) the change we want in our life must first begin within. That's true of anything you want in your life. For example, if you want to be in a relationship with someone who has certain qualities, embrace those qualities within yourself to live a new and abundant life.

Happiness Idea: *All lasting change starts within you first and then radiates outward.* The change you need can never be instilled on you from outside.

So, it's clear that happiness doesn't take any outside "thing." It doesn't take a new job, new relationship, more money, less money, more of anything or less of anything. I

f you believe your personal happiness revolves around these external influences you've become trapped into giving away your personal power and lowering your energy. And, a lower energy decreases the opportunities to connect with happiness.

Research studies show a portion of everyone's happiness is hardwired into us. That's just kind of the way we're individually "wired." But, these same studies also show *that you have control over the rest of your experience!* Let's put that number at around 40%.

The results of these studies revealed that 50% of how you feel is directly related to *how you choose to view what happens in your life!* So, research shows your perceptions control 50% of your life. Your perception is controlled by your personal history, your beliefs, biases, and your energy!

Happiness Idea: Only 10% of your happiness is determined by life circumstances such as employment, relationship status, or our financial situation.

But, What Do Most People Focus On?

It's hard to believe, but people spend nearly 100% of their vital life-energy feverishly trying to control the 10% that represents life circumstances! Think about that for a moment. People invest their vital life energy trying to control the 10% of life circumstances and *neglect spending time shaping the more influential 50% of the beliefs you can actually affect!*

Happiness Idea: This approach is backwards. Approaching life this way causes conflict within us that manifests outwards. This conflict then manifests as unhappiness. Thus, the end result is not surprising.

Now, think for a moment about what you believe is stopping you from being happy right now and in this moment? Maybe make a note to come back to this note later.

Balancing your life energy is one of the most important steps you can make to move forward into happiness. Life energy is the energy that surges through each of us. It's this energy that animates our lives. But living in this type of energy does require a certain level of consciousness and an awareness of our thoughts and beliefs for us to completely access and bring forward a new life experience.

Sometimes connecting with this energy is difficult when we're dealing with our own day-to-day muck. Yet, when we cultivate this energy, our lives begin to radiate joy outward. This flow can indicate whether we have balanced our center and are in-tune with ourselves or whether we are still stuck in a different experience.

Throughout history different cultures used various words to describe this energy. Some of these words are: Qi, matrix, morphic resonance, quantum energy fields, God, and many other names. The name is not important.

Lucky for us, these cultures spent thousands of years developing practices that allow us to tap into this energy for our lives.

Many ancient wisdoms share a common core belief that personally developing our awareness that all around us, every minute of every day, energy comes from our internal thoughts even though the world bombards us with outside influences. This internal energy surrounds and permeates our bodies influencing our health, thoughts, and happiness.

Even amid the cacophony of this bombardment by the external world, we can radiate our own internal energy outwards. Where does this mindset and energy come from? This energy is based on your thoughts and perceptions and your physical, spiritual, and emotional states in each moment.

Happiness Idea: These energy fields are intertwined in an ever-changing flux of thoughts, emotions, and positive and negative choices, and these finally coalesce into the creation of your personal energy "vibe" that represents who you are and how you exist in the world.

Your Path to Happiness

Happiness Idea: You start on the path to happiness by first becoming consciously aware that your interaction with this life energy (no matter what you name it) directly relates to your experience of happiness. If you are connected to self, the ability to experience true happiness is amplified, if you are disconnected from self, well, the chances of feeling happy are greatly diminished.

Many of us are disconnected from our center, so an important step is to integrate mindfulness practices that assist us to gently move forward into harmony with our center. This process is one of the most powerful steps to change our life.

Happiness Idea: Consider this-when your energy is blocked by fear, regret, remorse, worry, distractions, ruminating about the past, or dreading the future you are not balanced and, without this balance the experience of happiness escapes you.

But, is that all we need to do? Simply develop a mindfulness practice and then happiness awaits?

Nope, this doesn't mean just because you're connected to your center that everything goes smoothly in life- it doesn't. What it does mean is that even when things are rough and not flowing smoothly, when you are in this state of flow you more easily meet the challenges presented. As your life energy comes into balance, you experience more peace, contentment, and a youthful joy in life.

Happiness Idea: Through my experience with clients I have seen that as they incorporate some of the concepts here, that they begin to return to a more natural state of being: to exist in awe, wonder, joy, and happiness. Instead we're mired in the crap, the mundane, the down, the drive, and everything else we've been trained to do by society.

So, to counter the intentions of society you must intentionally see to balance your life energy, and this must be incorporated as a regular part of your day. Your life-balance must be given as much attention as work, eating and sleeping for you to experience more happiness.

Happiness Idea: You experience 50,000 thoughts a day but it's the thoughts you ***pay attention to*** that greatly determine whether you'll experience happiness.

You know, if happiness could be found in dealing with the distracting and familiar thoughts that surge through us every day no one would exist in a state of unhappiness. Your thoughts about the checkbook, your drive, what pants to wear, makeup etc. would disappear. But that's now how we are wired. We focus on what we are familiar (comfortable) with even if those thoughts do not serve us. So, how could the answer be found in dealing with those distraction when you have 50,000 or more thoughts a day? They can't!

So, you must develop a new skill- develop the ability to ask yourself good questions. And, one of the most important questions to learn to ask yourself during the day, is "why am I choosing to pay attention today to that particular thought?" Determine why are you focusing on those thoughts. What are you getting out of that experience? More of the same- a sense of comfort in the familiarity of your usual thoughts?

Most clients have become habituated to having (and reacting to) the same repetitive thoughts day after day. Then, they have the same reactions and feel the same way. This uninterrupted consistency of your thoughts creates a regular pattern of thinking and pattern of thinking feels like the real "you" because this is how you were yesterday and how you'll feel tomorrow.

But, this does not have to be the case.

This patterned stimulus-response can be interrupted with awareness. Instead of accepting these thoughts as "you", challenge these familiar thoughts merely as the habituated and unconscious internal response you've developed over the years. Because of this, you can change your response.

Happiness Idea: You're never going to "think" yourself happy (although there is often a sense of satisfaction from accomplishing the important tasks in your life. Why can't you think yourself happy? Because happiness is not experienced from the rational, logistical, thinking, "left-brained mind."

Happiness doesn't come from this mind/ego place of comparing, contrasting, competing and conceptions but comes from the place of consciousness and awareness. Let's talk about this a little more.

The Mind/Ego (Living From ME)

The parts of you that consist of mind/ego and consciousness are two different aspects of self. Many people fail to realize the subtle but important difference between the two. Mixing up these two models contributes to the experience of unhappiness so, let's look at their differences.

The beauty of your **mind/ego** is its excellence at working out the logistics necessary for day-to-day living. Balancing a check book is mind/ego. Driving somewhere by map this is mind/ego. Writing down your shopping list- mind/ego too. Problems occur when you are driven through life with a majority of your actions from either the mind or the ego.

Om the other hand is **a holistic awareness of consciousness** this connects your intuition with an expanded view of the world and is both a chosen perspective and a way of acting. Consciousness will bring you closer to happiness while existing solely within the mind/ego pushes you further away.

Illustrated throughout this book are tips and reminders that show how you can release the mind/ego control state to embrace the state of flow. There are methods to harmonize yourself so that your energy fields are balanced. From this center, you experience a greater sense of happiness.

Being centered and creating a vision is the state that allows you to see and create a vision of a balanced and harmonious life energy that embraces you-- in all aspects of your life. When you develop this ability to live more from your center you greatly increase your capacity to connect with the positive energy in yourself and within others. This connection to positive energy affects every aspect of your life, from your health and emotional state to your career and your relationships- and, happiness.

Happiness Idea: Your life energy affects you on the cellular level. This energy influences your life to a level you may have never imagined. This influence is so strong that our cellular DNA can be changed by these thoughts and actions!

The field of epigenetics. Science is finally catching up to this effect with the science of epigenetics which examines how life-style changes affect you daily considers how are life-choices, including the energy that we live in affect us.

Here's an example for you to consider how powerful this energy force is. Identical twins, twins who start out with identical DNA at birth, often develop different tangents and results through life that are vastly different as they age. The energy they lived in throughout their lives, energy they have created, been exposed to, or both, changed their outcomes projected over time.

Happiness Idea: Do not ignore your emotions and their messages. Chronic unhappiness indicates you're out of balance.

Happiness Idea: One contributor to this unbalanced state is the societal ingrained belief and resistance to understanding that there is no "there" needed for you to experience happiness.

Happiness already exists within you. Remember, that it's often not a new job, promotion or some other external achievement that's the answer. Those are often a temporary shot of adrenaline that alleviates. Pain for a moment. Yet, there is subtlety here- is your present job contributing to unhappiness? They by all means change it! Is a promotion an avenue to you fully expressing your genius and you are stifled at present? Then go for it? You must develop an emotional acuity and awareness to differentiate between goals for goals sake and goals for a fully gratifying experience of life. This subtlety presents is one of the most difficult concepts to experiencing more happiness in your life because it flies in the face of what most of us learn growing up.

Happiness Idea: To get to this moment, on this day, you have been taking part in a journey- your journey-that presents your personal life lessons and experiences. Each point in your life has been a part of a trip- your life journey. Are you enjoying this process as it unfolds? Are you waiting to get to the "there" before you allow happiness into your life?

With all the mental and emotional static in the world, and the internal static within us, we lose our way down the path that fits us. We get caught up with the latest, greatest something. This "caught up in" state or its companion state the "comparison mind-set" is another reason why you feel unhappy. Simply learn to pay attention to the feeling and don't try to suppress it with some dysfunctional behavior. It's just a feeling. The feelings you experience may be providing a warning, a beacon, to let you know you need to shift. They are there to assist you by telling you that something isn't right, and you need to do something different to get rebalanced, refocused, and in tune. This intuitive sense of well-being is the compass (your personal GPS) needed to guide you on your life journey.

Evaluation and judgement: As you experience different situations in life, your mind evaluates and judges each situation with your personal filters, beliefs, biases, and perspectives, all of which are based on your previous personal experience.

Happiness Idea: Each of us unconsciously apply our personal filters to match **our** preconceived ideas in a never-ending cycle of justifying exactly what we expect to see. If these perspectives allow happiness to flow through you, you experience happiness in many different situations. If not, you miss out.

Move out of the survival state. You're not meant to exist in the struggle/survival state of being- although those experiences are a part of life. You're not meant to be living just watching others enjoy their lives while you drag on in the daily grind. You're meant to really thrive—and to thrive you must move to a higher level of energy! Embracing an energetic shift to a frequency and higher energy brings more in your health, relationships, finances, and life! This energetic shift connects you with the vibrations of happiness and love. You aren't meant to exist in a sub-optimal state.

Happiness Idea: As we move through life if we haven't developed a method of clearing the negativity that we all deal with everyday this negativity can pull us down.

Becoming aware of the unrecognized buildup of negative energy is another important step towards allowing happiness. The accumulated effects of negativity are very subtle—building up slowly over years. If you don't pay attention, you will eventually exist in the lower energy states of depression. This translates into a low level of life energy. Any negative unconscious choice you make in your health, nutrition, relationships, career, affects you for life.

Happiness Idea: Experiencing happiness doesn't mean there aren't other emotions. Nor does it mean that you ignore your emotions. In fact, an integrated, holistic person learns to embrace emotions as the messengers. These emotional notifications indicate how well you are paying attention to yourself. When you are chronically unhappy, you are ignoring some (most) of your important emotional signals.

You must learn to care for your emotional and spiritual being. There's lots of tools to help you become energetically balanced (stop by the website donnenninger.com which has some meditations to address these types of imbalances). One meditation harmonizes your energy and the other meditation brings you to a higher energy level.

The Limits of Our Upbringing

Each person's upbringing places a limit on their exposure to the world. Thus, there's always more in life than you ever experience—and this is true for all of us. Being born into one system-- and this system may be your family, your education, your village, your religion, your political affiliation, your geographic location, or one of hundreds of other systems by nature excludes certain experiences from your life, unless you go and find them.

Happiness Idea: To experience more in your life, you must learn to step outside your original system to expand your knowledge and comfort zone. Until you do this, you continue to exist within the predefined limitations of each particular system you were raised in. The worst part about systems is that they rarely honor you. This is an awful because it doesn't allow tapping into the abundance of life that exists all around us. These are limits that can also limit your experience of happiness.

There're many times when a system serves and aligns with you, when that happens well, that's great because then there is no conflict. But, when the system does not align with you, conflict exists within you.

Happiness Idea: Ask yourself if you're willing to challenge yourself and expand your comfort zone to increase your energy level and embrace happiness?

Remember, emotions are not something you "get," emotions are something you experience. You do not get love; you are love. You do not "get" happy; you experience happiness.

Happiness Idea: You allow yourself to experience happiness, joy, and love because you **choose** to tune into the experience of them. These emotions are always available for you because they do not exist "out there." You experience all emotions energetically rather than "getting" them, happiness included.

There's lots of way that this effect is noticeable in life. Think about the different ways your tuning into what you'll allow into your awareness.

For example, maybe you bought a car and the same day you drive down the road you suddenly notice the same car everywhere? There are not suddenly more of these cars. You've tuned into seeing that car because of your heightened awareness. Or, is there a song that reminds you of someone you're missing and then you hear that song all the time? Same idea.

The above examples provide an idea of how experiencing happiness works; you see more of what you focus on. So, what you must focus on is creating a more powerful and uplifting energy through your thoughts and experiences. If your energy is low and sub-optimal, your experience of life is going to be low and sub-optimal.

The 7 Energetic Shifts to move into Happiness:

1. **Stop chasing happiness**. No matter how much you chase happiness, without the right energy you will never "find" it. Thus, happiness is not a thing you attain through external manifestations. Happiness is an energetic state you cultivate, grow, and expand **and** available for you.

2. **Remember that happiness is always, and only, available Now!**

3. **Happiness is not found in the external.** You can chase happiness through external achievement(s) but these achievements will never magically produce happiness. If you're on the right path- the journey is the source of your happiness. Do not buy into the idea that you get happy at your "destination" whatever that destination is for you.

4. **There is no "there."** Don't put off the experience of happiness until you get "there" (relationship, promotion, etc....) allow happiness during the process so that if you never get "there" you've enjoyed yourself on your path pursuing a life that is interesting to you.

5. **Money doesn't manifest happiness**. Happiness and abundance have nothing to do with material wealth. Nor does happiness relate to external manifestations of wealth.

6. Changing perspectives is the key. Happiness and abundance have everything to do with your energy, your beliefs, and your perspective.

7. Nurture your internal health. Happiness, abundance, and love are internal states of mind that appear in your life when you believe they are available in your life. Your energy must be available to the experience.

The Gratifying Life

As you fully actualize your life, a satisfaction warms your inner core. This is known in positive psychology as a gratifying experience. Gratifying experiences embrace your holistic being and indicate you are energetically balanced- this is living in happiness.

You've heard of people, athletes, performers talk about being "in the zone?" These experiences are the result of a balanced energy field, focus and immersion.

Here are some indicators to help you notice if you're in your zone.

Do you feel in harmony while engaged in a task?

Do you feel challenged to use skills you enjoy?

Do these challenges involve working on clear goals?

Do you feel like you have a sense of control?

Does your sense of self vanish?

Does time seem to stop?

When you cultivate these types of experiences for your life, rather than material items or status symbols, you contribute greatly to your happiness. Living this way is the result of a balanced energy state.

Think about it—doesn't having clear goals that have meaning to you indicate you're feeling in balance? Doesn't being so involved in something that time seems to stop indicate that you're engaging your holistic being—doesn't that indicate that your energy is balanced?

Happiness Idea: Embrace life through gratifying experiences. **Create** or discover the type of experiences that are soul-satisfying because if you don't, they you'll look for different ways to fill yourself and for most people these other ways are life-diminishing.

For some people, filling themselves with these other types of non-gratifying experiences may lead to an over-immersion in work while for others they may turn to maladjusted coping behaviors like booze and drugs. Others will try to relieve this hollowness through filling their life with relationships, believing other people can fill the emotional holes that exist within them. In this instance, you think their love can heal your pain and mistakenly believe if they love you "enough" then you will be okay. This hole (that we haven't yet learned to fill for ourselves) fuels a never-ending quest to meet our needs through others. That's a sure-fire recipe for unhappiness and the source of much relationship conflict.

Stop continuing dysfunctional coping behaviors. Turn to discover what old emotional wounds you carry that are restricting your energy flow and vitality. When you have emotional pain from yesterday that you still carry with you today, you're energetically blocked.

These emotional holes are internal energy blocks that can't be fixed from the outside; you must heal them from the inside to restore your balance today.

Think of your energy as a flowing river and any unresolved emotional pain as a dam that interrupts the flow of the river. Your internal dams are no less real than those dams that exist in the physical, three-dimensional world. And, if you want "flow" in your life, you must turn your attention to acknowledging and removing these dams. As you resolve them you will experience a dramatically improved energy flow in your life.

Relationships as fillers. Keep in mind too that a relationship, or your search for a relationship, sometimes serves the purpose of distracting you from your emotional "holes." This distraction is powerful—you know how unhappy you feel. But paying attention to and clearing the emotional resistance provides a better foundation for love and happiness rather than living from a subconscious psychological drive to avoid the pain of the emotional holes each of us has.

Happiness Idea: We often past project and/or future project about our lives and relationships. Is this true for you?

Remember that thoughts you have of the past and future are only projections of the mind. When you view your future with hope, you're excited. If you view your future with despair, you worry. Yet, neither condition yet exists; except in the mind. Learn to bring your focus and energy into the Now! When you truly embrace the idea that you live in the Now! And that you always have the Now! You open immediately to the possibility of the experience of happiness-Now!

Happiness Idea: Yes, I know, I can hear the argument- "If I don't save for my retirement, I'll be destitute. If I don't do this, that, or the other thing— than this, that, or the other thing will happen to me." For sure there are life-logistics to manage, but you can only take actions in the Now! You can only adjust and change in the Now!

Don't wait for "there." Have you ever stopped and reflected on how many people will still wait for their "there" to arrive before they think they will then allow the experience happiness to flow and that moment never arrives-it just never does- what a frustrating, wasteful experience of life they'll have with that mindset. Or, they get to the point they desired and realize how much they missed on the journey itself? That's a diminished experience of life.

Happiness Idea: How many people played by society's rules, rules they did not pick, and after 5, 10, or 20 years of effort waiting to get "there," to finally allow happiness into their lives, find themselves in an entirely new situation such as divorce, unemployment, or the death of a loved one? How many people will get a phone call that changes their life, perhaps finding a loved one is seriously ill?

Ask yourself-What is your "there?" What are you waiting for? What will it take before you will allow yourself to engage and fully enjoy life? Do you think it's a new relationship, job, money or something else? The belief that these items are a road to happiness is fake. So much of life is spent pursuing happiness rather than experiencing happiness in your pursuits.

Believe in the possibility of experiencing happiness in this moment and see where that perspective takes you **Live in the Now!** The desire for experiences like loving relationships, financial abundance, and good health are presenting the opportunity to develop them Now!

Remember too that happiness, like all emotions, is experienced in ebbs and flows. You don't have to be anything, or do anything, to experience everything.

Each emotion, each moment presents all opportunities for all experiences. Existing under the belief you should always be happy or always should be anything, lays the groundwork for chronic dissatisfaction.

Happiness Idea: Ask yourself if you unconsciously believe in the premise of **FLASH**- the **False Lesson You Always Should be Happy?**

If you've bought into this premise then you're going to spend your life chasing that feeling, rather than experiencing a feeling that will come naturally as you engage life more from your heart.

Experiencing happiness means you must challenge some pre-existing beliefs you carry, and this can be challenging. It is hard to awaken to the possibility that ideas, perspectives, and beliefs you've internalized as your "truth" simply represent the beliefs of one system, and that many other belief systems exist. That really is challenging because beliefs are all true and all false based on each person's perspective.

Examining and understanding the system you are born into helps to discover what beliefs you were exposed to at an early age. Discovering these beliefs really helps to allow you to start to align yourself with the ones that you truly resonate with.

Happiness Idea: A shortcut to information. Want a shortcut to recognize your energy level and your beliefs? Look at the results in your life present today. How do you feel today? Your life, as it exists today, is the result of what you thought and believed prior to today. If today's results are not what you envision for yourself, this dichotomy represents two things.

First, despite what you state you want consciously, you're living the life that represents what you

subconsciously believe you deserve or that you have been conditioned to accept.

Second, the results in your life indicate how close (or distant) from you're center you are living. The further away from your center, the more disharmony is present.

So, knowing this, it follows that any type of shift will bring change into your life. Choose changes that will bring an increase to your energy and, a new positive result that is what you want. Shift towards the experience of happiness. With new actions, more energy, and powerful beliefs you'll exist in a higher energy level, which is a happier place

Experiencing more happiness will certainly encompass cultivating gratifying life experiences but remember there's a big difference between filling your life with busy work and embracing situations that add to your life experience.

Pay attention to your intuitions. Allow yourself the freedom to follow your bliss. Consider what experiences provide truly gratifying experiences and find ways to connect with them. Limit those things causing discomfort and find ways to minimize exposure to them. Find people and situations you resonate with, and who connect with your true nature.

Avoid situations and people who are negative, or with whom you do not resonate.

Happiness Idea: Can you begin to see that the shift into happiness doesn't require dramatic effort? Start with a simple perspective shift. Start small and build on each of them, recognizing the ways each shift changes your life. As you become more internally connected, you will experience happiness because of being in a centered state of existence.

Get a bigger container for happiness! Hey, and while you're looking at happiness, check out the size of your happiness container. If your container for happiness is now small, choose a bigger container! Some people believe they only have a thimble for their happiness. Other believe they have a barrel to hold happiness. Finally, others believe they have unlimited access to the experience of happiness. You know what? In every case, they're each right. What they have conceived will be true. And if you want something different, you must shift your ideas.

Happiness Idea: Happiness only exists in the Now! There is only Now! There is only Now! There is only Now! The only moment you have control over is Now!

Remember that projections into the future, or remembrances of the past, are distractions of the mind/ego taking your energy away from this moment. The only moment available to you is Now!

Check to see if now, in this moment, you're wasting time comparing yourself to others. If so, you're creating a diminished energy and that's one way people ensure unhappiness- investing time and energy in comparison with others.

Happiness Idea: Why does this comparison paradigm add to people's misery? Because, we all possess a natural bias to overlook our good and overemphasize our self-perceived shortcomings. You judge things better or worse, forgetting that these are subjective evaluations.

Because of this bias, we selectively compare and project "on to" others only our selective (and mostly inaccurate) interpretation. By selectively comparing, you create an artificial structure that diminishes the uniqueness of your gifts. This perspective lowers your energy and a low energy level is a contributor to unhappiness.

Discover Your Happiness Rules!

Happiness Idea: Each of us has subconsciously incorporated arbitrary rules on what must happen to be happy. Then, we waste our life-energy jumping through these ridiculous "monkey hoops" of society's influence.

We lower our emotional health trying to check off these unknown boxes of our internalized happiness rules. Rules we don't know! Worse yet, we check the accomplishments off and wonder why we feel hollow and lacking.

Peoples' subconscious happiness rules frequently consist of something roughly like the following: "for me to be happy, I must have this, or I must have that, or I must have the other thing, then I will be happy." I wished that really worked because then happiness would be easy to achieve. All you would have to do is check off the formula and Boom! by following that formula and type of thinking everyone would be happy. But, we know that's not how happiness works!

Happiness Idea: Happiness comes from being fully present in the moment you are now in.

Self-reflect and see if you have a set of limiting conditions for happiness. You will often find that these rules are difficult to achieve, or your rules are focused on the "out there," thus, your ability to experience happiness is severely reduced.

Happiness Idea: Often, the above unknown rules are comingled with self-imposed subconscious expectations that people carry. Again, these impose a further hindrance to happiness. The more specific something must be for you to experience happiness, the more constrained your opportunities and the harder experiencing happiness is.

There is incredible power in releasing anger and resentment. Although for many people this release feels as if you're giving away your power, to experience more happiness in your life you must learn to release resentment and anger. The negative energy, past resentments and anger are energetically life draining- not life-enhancing! Ask yourself what possible good can holding on to these feeling do for you today? Ask too if it's possible to experience happiness and the fullness of life if your life is filled with resentment and anger? And really, the people or situations you are angry about or resent are not being affected by your feelings- you are.

To experience happiness now, your life cannot be filled with unresolved traumas or unfinished business from your past. Check out our website for a specific meditation for clearing old past experiences so that you can embrace the present to be energetically clear.

Why do people resist the idea of releasing resentment believing that their releasing resentment is implicit approval of someone's behavior or actions. They believe releasing anger and resentment is disempowering to them or is some form of approval of those situations which they are angry about. Others mistake the adrenaline rush of resentment and anger for true power and energy.

I suggest the opposite is true. Today, you burden yourself by carrying this load of resentment and anger from your past. If you refuse to release the past I guarantee you're paying the price in unhappiness today. The thoughts and actions that accompany the emotions of resentment and anger are energy depleting. There is no way that these energies affirm or positively influence your life.

Happiness Idea: As justified and righteous as anger and resentment feel for you, in this moment these feelings are only affecting *you*, they are a burden only for *you*, and the only one hurting about this, in the Now! is you.

Because of the intensity of these feelings, you may have put up an internal blockage, some type of wall, inside yourself. You think that living authentically today is dangerous and because of living behind this wall you've abandoned the deep connection with your spirit in this moment, and this moment is all we have.

Whatever experience caused anger and resentment to well up inside of you is over. By carrying these feelings today, you carry the negative energy vibration and you pay the price every day. Release these and live powerfully Now!

Release resentments and anger about your past or worry of the future to live fully in the now. To release them, you can't hide from them, you've got to fully process them by going through them and letting them go. The Happiness Recordings™ helps to resolve these old emotional wounds to release their impact. This way you're free to live in this moment with happiness, vitality, and love.

Learning to forgive a past situation that's contributing to your present resentment and anger is one of the wonderful contributions that churches and other spiritual organizations provide for their parishioners. They understand that for you to live fully in the now, you must release resentments and anger about your past or worry of the future. You can't hide from them, you've got to fully process them by going through them and letting them go.

The Happiness Recordings™ helps to resolve these old emotional wounds to release their impact. This way you're free to live in this moment with happiness, vitality, and love.

Your ability to forgive, grow, and learn from your experiences frees up more space for happiness.

Happiness Idea: Churches realized long ago that having a group of low energy, low resonating parishioners is not good for the world and certainly doesn't embrace all you are. Thus, they make forgiveness one of the cornerstones of their belief systems-and forgiveness is a powerful antidote to resentment and anger.

For your health and happiness, forgive today and reclaim the joyful and youthful energies that are already in you but covered by these powerful energy inhibitors.

Create opportunities for fun! Having fun is another way you reset your energy levels. Think about it for a moment—if you are not having fun, you are living in some type of energetic stress. Just because you have become acclimated to a life without fun and joy doesn't mean that this is good for your spirit. This stress you experience can be due to many legitimate factors; a job you hate, a relationship that is unloving, poor choices about how you honor yourself, unhealthy food and lifestyle choices. In each, these lower your life energy.

Learn to pay attention to flow and create a positive energy to experience a full life, find and embrace activities that allow fun to flow and for laughter to become an integrated part of your holistic being. Happiness, laughing, and enjoying life are absolute necessities to reset your spiritual center.

Take the time to balance yourself energetically, you will allow yourself to enter each moment today present rather than dragging along some pre-existing emotional pain. Look, in many societies they tell you that to experience happiness, go have another drink, eat another doughnut, take an antidepressant, go flirt on Facebook, or use some other dysfunctional behavior. Not going to work!

Happiness Idea: As society exists today, relentlessly driving yourself towards an eventual heart attack is a badge of honor. Having fun, being balanced, avoiding the heart attack by embracing (and enjoying) life is not socially accepted and is often frowned on as unacceptable (to them) behavior.

Society deems it more acceptable to have a heart attack, and then spend a fortune recovering, rather than avoiding a heart attack (or anxiety, depression, or any other illness) through balancing your energy, joy, awareness, and consciousness. That's just an illusory choice- step outside that choice.

Because society does not encourage you to run, enjoy a spa, go to a game, take a class, camp, golf, read, meditate, or engage in experiences that reduce the chance of illness and increase the quality of your life you must invest in yourself and nurture these parts of you.

Some clients have found it interesting to look at life with a cost benefit analysis to your life choices. For those of you familiar with business, you know that a cost-benefit analysis is an examination of long-term benefits compared with the short-term costs. This analysis often reveals how assets can be used most effectively to produce a positive result even if there is a short-term cost involved.

These clients relate to looking at life as important as business and have found that by not making important daily short-term investments, the long-term cost is very high. They pay a price in life dissatisfaction and poor health. Isn't this something you're already intuitively aware of?

Happiness Idea: One of the enjoyable explorations in life is discovering things that provide you deep pleasure. But, for many of us choosing to experience pleasure at this level is an outlandish concept.

So instead, we exchanged our ability to enjoy this deep pleasure by substituting some type of dysfunctional, short-term, state changing replacements such as smoking, alcohol/drug use, dysfunctional relationships and other energy lowering behaviors.

This avoidance of deep pleasure is harmful. To recharge your spirit, cultivate experiences that fully engage you.

Think back for a moment and see when you have felt the difference in your energy when you are in the zone of true happiness.

Connection with the Positive- People and Places

Happiness Idea: You can create an energetic harmony in your life by participating in activities that connect with positive energy- makes sense, right?

Throughout the centuries cultures have talked about different expressions of this energy and ways that you can connect with it daily. The following suggestions will help you begin to reconnect with the positive energy you need to increase your experience of happiness.

Use water for clearing. When you bathe, shower, swim, walk in the weather, and other experiences that connect you with the Earth and water you shift to a higher energy level. Water is a very healing energy therapy.

Become harmonious with the earth, for example by walking barefoot through your lawn, or going for a walk at the beach or in the woods. Each of these are powerfully simple ways to reconnect with grounding energy.

Meditations, hypnosis, visualizations, and deep breathing are types of exercises that allow you to remove yourself from the chaos and cacophony of life, helping you to reestablish a connection with your simple and pure being. On our website are many powerful modalities to assist you to bringing your center back into energetic harmony.

Physical exercise and incorporating physical effort in life are wonderfully powerful ways to rebalance your energy. Going out into the snow or into a spring rain connects you with the earth and harmonizes your energy.

Take a drive or short walk when you are low on physical energy. Going somewhere beautiful helps to reconnect you with your energy.

Trying something new to break out of your rut. This opens your brain to the development of new neural pathway development and this can shift your energy dramatically!

Contemplate the "unthinking actions" you take each day. How do you handle coming home from work—do you put on the TV news and let all the negativity sold by mass media subtly influence you?

Change your routine and change your environment to a more positive vibe. This allows connection to the energy fields on a different and more empowering level!

Experiment with different energy modalities to realign your core or chakras. Try massage, Qi Gong, Reiki therapy, acupuncture, and other Eastern energy balancing therapies.

Consider other therapies that will help your balancing such as sound healing, EFT, EMDR, bilateral stimulation, brainwave entrainment, different therapies and personal coaching can help you to clear out old blockages and thus increase your energy.

Begin to take any of the many simple actions mentioned in this book to increase your energy level and feel more in harmony.

Simplify your life. Another powerful and simple set of actions involves simplifying your life. Do you really need a new car, more electronics, and other expensive gifts that require huge investments in time, effort and your energy?

Connect with people and activities that are conscious and positive. Look for and find ways to connect with people who are living in consciousness and who want to share positive energy with you? Where will you find these people?

Giving- find a way to share with others by giving. Take them out for a cup of coffee. Just give someone who needs it a $5 or $10. Although this amount is small, the benefits to you, the giver are enormous!

Nurture yourself with sleep. This is hard for so many people because they have become desensitized to their natural circadian rhythms. Fluorescent lights, time changes, long hours, medicines, each of these and more disturbs our natural flow. Make a focus to start making sleep a sanctuary for you. Lights off, white noise (or no noise) on, no electronics, consistency, TV off, no computers and just be. The shift will take a while, but it will occur. This way, you're not entering the next day in a low-flow state.

Find a way to give of yourself. Not with money this time, but with effort and connection. You can receive enormous benefit by giving of yourself. The act of giving takes you away from the immediacy of your concerns and issues and lets a new place develop as you share.

Simplify and clean. Look, no one ever said they were happier with more complications and more stress in their life. That said, the easiest thing to do is clean your physical space. Desk, home, work area- you don't have to be obsessive, just organized- organized feels better. Same with the other things in your life- where can you simplify- then do it!

Pay attention to the foods you put into your body. Consider the amounts of caffeine, refined sugar, and processed foods that have already affected you. There great benefits in nurturing foods- herbal and green teas, deep dark chocolates, not proceed food. When you make this change and combine it with the others outlined here you physically start to change- and to feel better and more alive.

Remember not to compare where you are today with anyone or anything- even yourself. Remember FLASH it's a false belief. Simply appreciate where you are at in this moment on this day!

Pay attention to your intuition to see what really resonates with you. Find people that are positive. Find activities that are centered on an energy that enhances your DNA rather than damaging it.

Reconnect-Energy connects you with your heart and brings you deeper into a state of satisfaction and happiness. Do you believe it's possible to be happy if your head and your heart are disconnected? Of course, not—yet that's how many of us exist. This heart-head connection is your guide to abundance, love, balance, and energetic happiness. You do not ignore life's logistics, you simply rebalance and exist in a different and more positive energy field, and this produces dramatically different results!

Experience space-time slippage- Have you had any experience that brings you to a space where time seems to stop because you are so engaged in the moment that the past and future cease to exist? This is ultimate happiness and this type of activity restores and balances your spirit. Embrace these experiences! Don't delay a minute longer!

Be aware that the energy, thoughts and beliefs that you bring into each situation constantly affects your view of current external circumstances. You can only see what you are capable of seeing in this moment. How you view these circumstances creates your feelings. The internal associations you carry are under your control and you can change them to better support you. Blaming others for how you feel, or where you find yourself today, delays your growth. You cannot experience happiness if you blame other people for how you feel.

Create Consciousness-This presents another powerful reason to focus on living authentically and to be balanced energetically. You can be happier, live more abundantly, be healthier, and more content if you choose to create a life of consciousness that pays as much attention to your energetic needs as it does to your physical and physiological needs.

Follow your bliss and pay attention to intuition! The following study is a simple example that shows how following your bliss leads to the manifestation of abundance by people who have chosen to create their lives based on their inner truth. The results of a study performed years ago on a group of millionaires provided startling information about how enjoying life transfers into the real world. Fifteen hundred people had been divided into two groups: A and B. Group A, consisted of 1400 people, who worked first for money and then did what they loved. Group B, consisted of 100 people who did what they loved. In other words, they followed their bliss. Years later, an astounding discovery was made. All the millionaires (except one) came from Group B, the group that did what they loved!

Pay attention to the signs of harmony and disharmony. You simply can't be balanced if you exist in a state of disharmony and when you're not following your bliss—you're in a state of disharmony. Get your energy clear and cared for, and then abundance follows. This is true in relationships, finances, and business. This is not theory; this is fact!

Resolve or reframe old experiences to increase the amount of happiness, financial freedom, and abundance you have in life. Think about how important this is. Would your financial situation improve if you were in tune, in harmony, energetically balanced, and more aware of your intuitions? You bet it would! Would the quality of your relationships improve with more empowering beliefs? Of course! If you stay in the Now! and give yourself the attention you need you will experience more happiness!

Believe you are worthy of happiness and abundance. Remember your present experience reveals only the limited range you are aware of today. As you grow your experiences and awareness also grow and you will begin to see and to believe that more is available for you.

Choose gratefulness. Of course, even after your energy is balanced and in-flow, there are moments that you are not experiencing happiness and you would like to shift your energy to cultivate this state. A powerful exercise you can do in these moments it to keep a gratitude journal.

According to the results of a study done by *Emmons and McCollough in 2003,* people who keep gratitude journals feel better about their lives compared with the population that did not keep the journal. Those who kept the journal found themselves to be more optimistic about the upcoming week compared to those who recorded life hassles or neutral life events.

Write down what you're grateful for. This action is a really simple step that is proven to help you feel better about life. When you feel better you have better energy, and when you have better energy you open to the experience of happiness! Keep a gratitude journal. Stop chasing happiness. Balance your energy and allow happiness to flow through you.

Find your path. All day you make decisions that either increase your positive connection to yourself or keep you living in disharmony. My wish for you is that you find **your path** to living in the energy of consciousness and awareness.

You may be surprised at how much abundance and happiness have always been available for you! **This book lays a positive foundation** for the process of living in a field of positive energy AKA happiness.

When you experience an increase in harmony, you balance and increase your energy. This increases your ability to experience happiness in a pure way rather than attempting to "get happy" through some short-tern dysfunctional coping behavior that is a numbing and energy lowering experience.

By now you've noticed this book was not filled with grandiose ideas and impossible concepts. Instead, this book is filled with small shifts and thankfully, these shifts are completely in your control. The biggest change in the world comes not from massive external change, but from how you **choose to view** what is already there. This is what being energetically balanced is about—making decisions that are harmonious for your soul, that resonate with your spirit, that physically invigorate you, that brings vitality into your life, and connects you with the vital pure essence that is the core of your being.

How Happy Will You Allow Yourself To Be?

Peace and happiness! Don

Check out our website to read more about how to create a truly abundant life and read Don's most recent book!

And remember, as we started:

People are as happy as they make up their minds to be. ~Abraham Lincoln.

And

You are what you think you are. ~Buddha

www.ingramcontent.com/pod-product-compliance
Lightning Source LLC
Chambersburg PA
CBHW060208260726

48658CB00005BA/1945